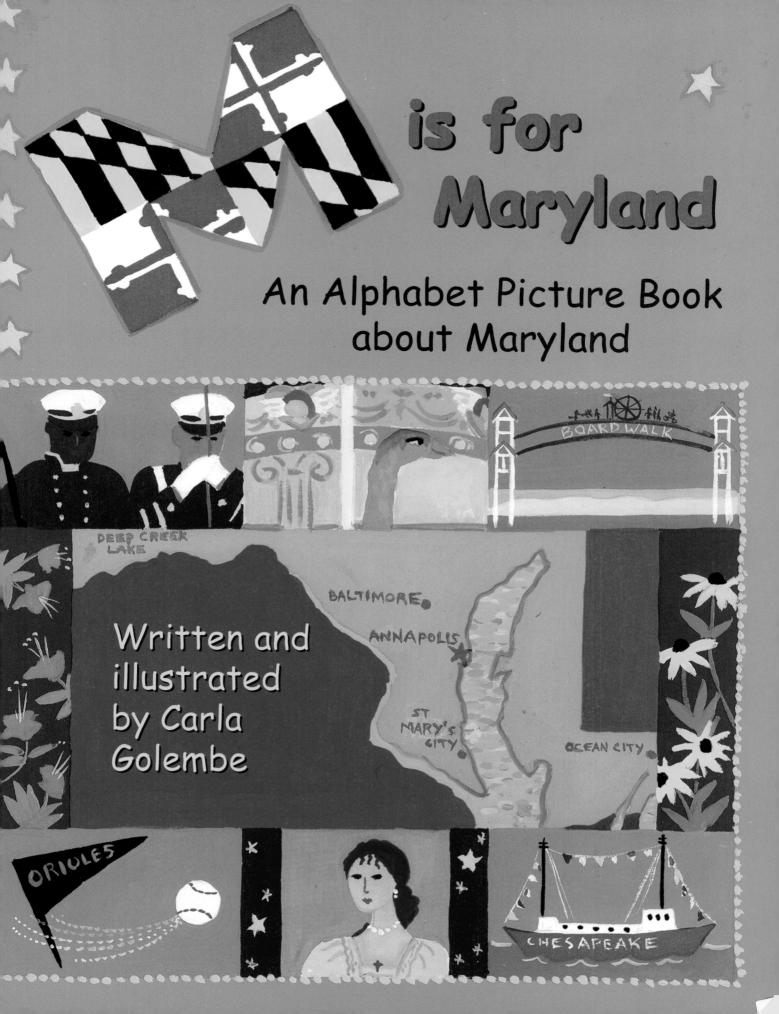

M is for Maryland

An Alphabet Picture Book about Maryland

Written and illustrated by Carla Golembe

BOARD WALK

DEEP CREEK LAKE

BALTIMORE

ANNAPOLIS

ST MARY'S CITY

OCEAN CITY

ORIOLES

CHESAPEAKE

Other books about *Very Special Places* from VSP Books:

Woodrow, the White House Mouse, about the presidency and the nation's most famous mansion.

Woodrow For President, about how Woodrow got to the White House.

House Mouse, Senate Mouse, about Congress and the legislative process.

Marshall, the Courthouse Mouse, about the Supreme Court and the judicial process.

A "Mice" Way to Learn About Government teachers curriculum guide, for the three books above.

A "Mice" Way to Learn about Voting, Campaigns and Elections teachers curriculum guide, for *Woodrow for President.*

Capital Cooking with Woodrow and Friends, a cookbook for kids that mixes fun recipes with fun facts about American history and government.

Alexander, the Old Town Mouse, about historic Old Town, Alexandria, Va., across the Potomac River from Washington, D.C.

Nat, Nat, the Nantucket Cat, about beautiful Nantucket Island, Mass.

Martha's Vineyard, about wonderful Martha's Vineyard, Mass.

Cornelius Vandermouse, the Pride of Newport, about historic Newport, R.I., home to America's most magnificent mansion houses.

Mosby, the Kennedy Center Cat, based on the true story of a wild stage cat that lived in the Kennedy Center in Washington D.C.

Order these books through your local bookstore by title,
by calling 1-800-441-1949, or from our website at www.VSPBooks.com.

For a brochure and ordering information, write to:

VSP Books
P.O. Box 17011
Alexandria, VA 22302

To get on our mailing list, send your name and address to the address above.

Text and illustrations © 2000 by Carla Golembe

ISBN 1-893622-03-7

Library of Congress Catalog Card Number: 00-134785

10 9 8 7 6 5 4 3 2 1

Printed in the United States of America

For Rita Cacas, Carol Ostrow
and Liz Rees, who welcomed
me to Maryland.

—C.G.

A is for **Annapolis**. Annapolis is the capital of Maryland. The Governor and General Assembly work there to create the laws that everyone in the state lives by. The General Assembly is made up of the Senate and the House of Delegates. A is also for **azalea**. Azaleas bloom in bright pink and red and purple and white in Maryland in the spring.

B is for **Black-eyed Susan**, the state flower. Black-eyed Susans grow in gardens and fields and along roadsides throughout the state. B is also for Baltimore, which was named for Lord Baltimore, who governed Maryland in colonial times.

C is for **crabs** and **Chesapeake**. Maryland blue crabs come from the Chesapeake Bay. Blue crabs are the state crustacean and are wonderful food. Maryland sells more blue crabs to families and restaurants than any other state. Sometimes they are made into crab cakes, which are delicious.

D is for Frederick **Douglass** (1818-1895), who was a great orator and African-American leader. He was born in Easton. He fought against slavery all of his life. D is also for **Deep Creek Lake**, Maryland's largest inland body of water. It's located in Garrett County. It was formed by a dam, which provides electric power. Deep Creek Lake covers 4,000 acres. It's a great place for boating, fishing and camping.

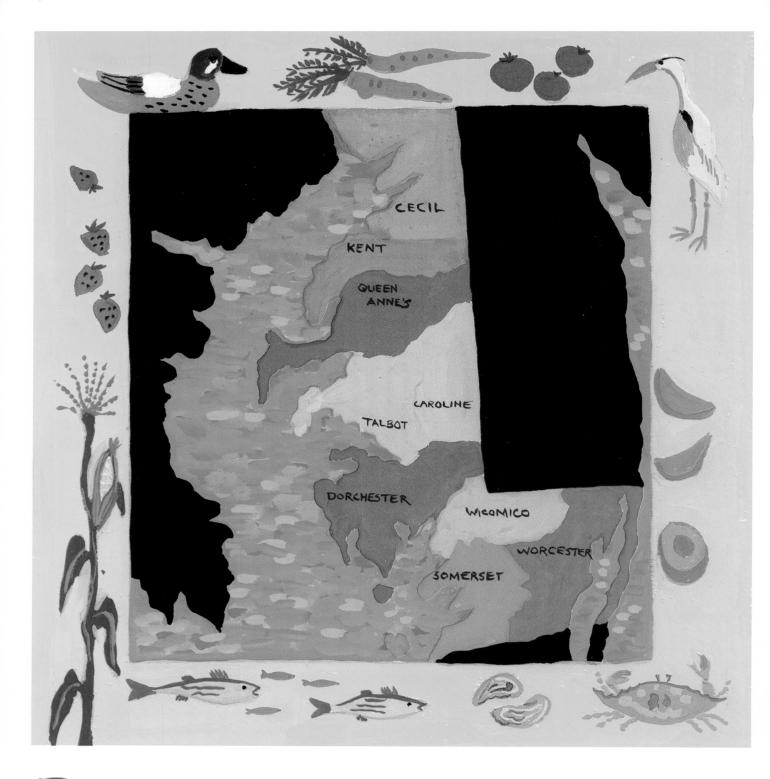

E is for **Eastern Shore**. That's the part of Maryland between the Chesapeake Bay and the ocean. If you explore the Eastern Shore, you will find many small towns and fishing villages, marshes and wildlife areas. Farmers grow melons, corn, strawberries, soybeans and vegetables there. Oysters, crabs and fish live in the waters of the Eastern Shore.

F is for **Flag**. The state flag of Maryland depicts the coat of arms of the Calvert family, which governed Maryland when it was an English colony. Cecil Calvert was also called Lord Baltimore. The King of England, Charles the First, appointed him to rule Maryland during colonial times.

G is for **Glen Echo Park**. In 1891, Glen Echo began as a "chautauqua," a place where people could learn about art, science and literature. By 1900, it was an amusement park. In 1971, it became a national park. On its grounds is the Dentzel Carousel, which is hand-carved and was built in 1921. It has 40 horses, four rabbits, four ostriches, a giraffe, a deer and a lion. Which animal would you like to ride on?

H is for **historic St. Mary's City**, which was the first capital of Maryland, before Annapolis. St. Mary's City is located in southern Maryland. It was the first place in America where people could attend whatever place of worship they chose, helping to establish our nation's tradition of freedom of religion. Today, it is a living history and archaeological museum and a National Historic Landmark.

I is for **Inner Harbor**. Many office buildings, shops, hotels and restaurants
line Baltimore's Inner Harbor. The Maryland Science Center, Port Discovery,
the Baltimore Maritime Museum and the National Aquarium are there, too. Events
at the stadiums at Camden Yards and the Convention Center bring lots of visitors

to the Inner Harbor. The water taxi takes passengers all along the Inner Harbor to historic Fells Point. (There are many other wonderful museums in Baltimore, such as the Maryland Historical Society and the Eubie Blake National Jazz Institute and Cultural Center.)

J is for **jousting**, the official state sport of Maryland. Jousters are people who ride horses toward each other and try to knock each other down with a long pointed pole called a lance. Jousting was a form of dangerous combat performed

by knights hundreds of years ago. Today, you can see jousting for fun at the Maryland Renaissance Faire every fall and at the state jousting championships held from August through October.

K is for Francis Scott **Key** (1779-1843). Key, who was born in Frederick, was inspired to write "The Star-Spangled Banner" in 1814 after the British bombed Fort McHenry in an attempt to capture Baltimore. They did not succeed. Congress adopted the song as our national anthem in 1931. The Star-Spangled Banner Flag House, where Mary Pickersgill made the flag that Key wrote about, is located in Baltimore.

L is for **lock**, a section of a waterway closed off with gates. There are 74 locks on the C & O Canal between Georgetown in Washington, D.C., and Cumberland, Maryland. The canal was completed in 1850. Each lock raised the water level by 8 feet, so that boats going over the waterfalls on the Potomac River could travel on a safe, steady waterway. L is also for **locomotives**. The Baltimore and Ohio Railroad (1828) was the first one in the Western Hemisphere to carry both freight and passengers.

benjamin banneker *eubie blake* * *
billie holiday *** cass elliot* dashiell
hammett * * matthew henson* *johns

PENNSYLVANIA

MARYLAND

DELAWARE

WEST VIRGINIA

VIRGINIA

hopkins ** edgar allen poe*gertrude
stein* upton sinclair* harriet tubman*
thurgood marshall edwin booth* **

M is for **Maryland**, the seventh state to enter the Union, on April 28, 1788. The state bird is the Baltimore Oriole. The state boat is the Skipjack. Many accomplished people from all walks of life came from Maryland. Do you know for whom Maryland is named? (See Q)

N is for United States **Naval Academy**, located in Annapolis. The Naval Academy is a four-year college that has trained young people to become professional officers in the U.S. Navy and Marine Corps since 1845. Students study the same subjects they would at any college but also learn all the aspects of seamanship and leadership. Graduates are called "midshipmen" or "middies." The Naval Academy has a museum with art and model ships and objects that relate to the traditions and history of the Navy.

O is for **Ocean City**. In the summer, when it gets really hot, many people head to this famous beach town on the Atlantic Ocean. The boardwalk there is always crowded and lively. From the top of the Ferris wheel, you can see way out

over the ocean to the horizon. And the best part is playing in the waves and picnicking on the beach. Everything tastes better at the ocean.

P is for **Potomac River**. The river is 400 miles long and flows from the mountains of West Virginia along the Maryland/Virginia border, through Washington, D.C., and back into Maryland where it meets the Chesapeake Bay at Point Lookout. There are many national parks and historic places along the river, including Harper's Ferry National Historical Park; the C & O Canal, with its many locks, and Great Falls. There are lots of places along the river to fish or kayak or hike.

Q is for **Queen Henrietta Maria**, who was the wife of King Charles the First of England. In 1632, Charles signed the charter for the Calvert family to establish the Maryland colony. In honor of the king, the Calverts named it for Henrietta Maria.

R is for Babe **Ruth** (1895-1948), one of the greatest baseball players who ever lived. He grew up in Baltimore and was from a poor family. The first team he played for was the Baltimore Orioles. He broke all records for home runs, runs batted in, runs scored and bases scored. During his career, he hit 714 homers. The Babe Ruth Birthplace and Orioles Museum is in Baltimore.

S is for **sailing**. On a sunny, breezy day, the Chesapeake Bay is full of boats of every size, shape and color. When you sail past the buoys, you might see ospreys nesting in them. And you also may see...

T is for **Thomas Point Lighthouse**. This lighthouse, which is located on Thomas Point Shoals near the South River, is a funny shape. It's a cottage-style "screwpile" lighthouse. From 1875 until 1986, it was operated by a person who lived in it. Now a computer runs it. Can you imagine living there surrounded by the sea?

U is for **USS Constellation**, the last surviving Civil War ship and the last warship that the U.S. Navy built that used only sails and no engines. She was launched in 1854. The Constellation has been restored and is docked in the Inner Harbor. U is also for **umbrella**. The first umbrella factory in the nation opened in Baltimore in 1828.

V is for the **American Visionary Art Museum**, which is located in Baltimore. Many artists whose work is shown there never went to art school. All the work is very personal, about dreams and feelings. Most of the artists use bright colors. Outside, there is a huge "whirligig," a big sculpture made of tree limbs that you can climb into, and there is a car covered with beads. Two other great art museums in Baltimore are the Baltimore Museum of Art and the Walters Art Gallery.

W is for the **War Between the States**, which is another name for the Civil War. Though Maryland sided with the Union, it was a border state during the Civil War. Battles between the Northern and Southern armies were fought in Maryland at South Mountain, Antietam and Monocacy. You can visit these famous battlefields.

X is for **xylophone**. Xylophones (balaphons), drums and folk instruments from all over the world can be found at the House of Musical Traditions, a store in Takoma Park. HMT also gives lessons and sponsors concerts. It has been a Takoma Park landmark since 1972.

Y is for **you** are here. On the map, you can find Maryland by following the arrows. Maryland is on the East Coast of the United States, in the mid-Atlantic region.

Z is for **Zippy** and **Zoe**. They are my cats and they live with me in Silver Spring, Maryland. They are both very affectionate and really smart. When they're not chasing fireflies, opening cabinets or hiding my keys, they like to sit on my worktable and watch me paint and write. They're here now.